GIANT OCEAN ANIMALS

# MANATEE

## Gentle Giant

BY EMMANUEL MARSHALL

Enslow PUBLISHING

**Please visit our website, www.enslow.com. For a free color catalog of all our high-quality books, call toll free 1-800-398-2504 or fax 1-877-980-4454.**

**Cataloging-in-Publication Data**
Names: Marshall, Emmanuel.
Title: Manatee / Emmanuel Marshall.
Description: Buffalo, NY : Enslow Publishing, 2027. | Series: Giant ocean animals | Includes glossary and index.
Identifiers: ISBN 9781978550681 (pbk.) | ISBN 9781978550698 (library bound) | ISBN 9781978550704 (ebook)
Subjects: LCSH: Manatees--Juvenile literature.
Classification: LCC QL737.S63 M377 2027 | DDC 599.55--dc23

Published in 2027 by
Enslow Publishing
2544 Clinton Street
Buffalo, NY 14224



Portions of this work were originally authored by Katie Chanez and published as *Manatees*. All new material in this edition was authored by Emmanuel Marshall.

Cover Designer: Joshua Olson
Interior Designer: Joshua Olson
Editor: Noah Riccardi

Photo Credits: Cover, p. 1 Greg Amptman/Shutterstock.com; pp. 4–5 tobiasfrei/iStockphoto; pp. 6–7 mpwoodib/iStockphoto; pp. 8–9 Melissa Burovac/Shutterstock.com; pp. 10–11 Windover Way Photography/Shutterstock.com; pp. 12, 16–17 somdul/Shutterstock.com; p. 13 Kent Weakley/Shutterstock.com; pp. 14–15 Peter Douglas Clark/Shutterstock.com; pp. 18–19 Andrea Izzotti/Shutterstock.com; pp. 20–21, 29 Natalie11345/Shutterstock.com; pp. 22–23 benedek/iStockphoto; pp. 24–25 Jeffery Edwards/Shutterstock.com; pp. 26–27 Erin Westgate/Shutterstock.com.



Printed in China



CPSIA compliance information: Batch #QS27ENS: For further information contact Enslow Publishing, at 1-800-398-2504.

# TABLE OF CONTENTS

CHAPTER 1

# ALL ABOUT MANATEES

Manatees are large **mammals** that live in water. They can be more than 13 feet (4 m) long. And they can weigh more than 3,500 pounds (1,588 kg).

**Manatees live in shallow waters near coasts.**

Manatees are **herbivores**. They eat water plants. Manatees use their front **flippers** to hold their food. They pull the food toward their mouths.

**Manatees can eat up to 130 pounds (59 kg) of food a day.**

## MANY TEETH

A manatee's teeth are all **molars**. New teeth grow in the back of its mouth. As the old teeth wear down, new ones slowly move forward to take their place.

Manatees may spend up to eight hours a day eating.

Manatees tend to move slowly. They spend most of their time resting or eating. They can reach 20 miles per hour (32 km/h) for a short period of time. However, they usually swim less than 5 miles per hour (8 km/h).

**Small hairs cover a manatee's body. They help manatees sense their surroundings.**

CHAPTER 2

# LIFE IN THE SHALLOWS

Like all mammals, manatees breathe air. They can stay underwater for up to 15 minutes. Then they come up to the surface to breathe.

**Manatees breathe through their nostrils. They close them underwater.**

Manatees usually live alone or in pairs. Sometimes they form small groups. The groups find places with a lot of food or warm water.

**Manatees eat more than 10 percent of their body weight in food each day.**

Groups of manatees often form in warm waters during winter.

A manatee can't bend its neck. It has to turn its whole body to look sideways.

Baby manatees can weigh 60 to 70 pounds (27 to 32 kg) when they are born.

Many manatee pairs are mothers and their young. Females usually have one baby every two or three years. In the wild, manatees can live to be almost 60 years old.

## EARLY LIFE

Baby manatees are called calves. At first, they **nurse** from their mothers. Later, they start eating plants. By age two, they leave their mothers to live on their own.

CHAPTER 3

# COASTAL CREATURES

Manatees live along coasts and in rivers. These waters are shallow. They get sunlight. As a result, lots of **algae** and water plants grow.

Manatees mainly eat seagrass.

Many manatees live near Florida and in the Caribbean Sea.

There are three types of manatees. One kind swims along the southeast coasts of North America. Another kind lives along West Africa. The third type lives in South America's Amazon River.

## MERMAID MANATEES

**Long ago, sailors claimed to see mermaids in the ocean. They likely saw manatees instead. Manatees sometimes stick their heads above water. And their flippers can look like hands.**

All these areas have warm water. Manatees can't live in places where the water is too cold.

**A manatee has three or four nails on each flipper.**

Some people call manatees sea cows.

CHAPTER 4

# DANGER TO MANATEES

Manatees have very few natural **predators**. Humans are manatees' biggest threats. For example, people build along the coast. These buildings can destroy manatees' **habitats**.

**A boat travels near a manatee in a Florida river.**

Signs warn boaters to watch out for manatees.

People also drive boats where manatees live. Manatees are slow swimmers. They cannot move away from boats quickly. Boats can hurt or kill manatees.

## OUT OF THE WAY

**Alligators occasionally eat manatee babies. But they mostly leave manatees alone. In fact, if they run into one another, the gators will swim out of the way.**

Tourists sometimes get to see manatees up close.

People are working to **protect** manatees. Manatees were once **endangered** in the United States. Now they are not.

**Some people have spotted hundreds of manatees swimming together as a group.**

# TEST YOUR KNOWLEDGE

*Take this quiz to test your knowledge.*

1. Write a sentence that describes the key ideas from Chapter 3.
2. Would you ever want to travel to see manatees? Why or why not?
3. What do manatees eat?
   - A. water plants
   - B. fish
   - C. alligators
4. Why do shallow waters get more sunlight than deeper waters?
   - A. Sunlight fades as it travels deeper into water.
   - B. Sunlight starts shining from the seafloor.
   - C. Sunlight gets stronger as it travels deeper into water.

**5.** What does **occasionally** mean in this book?

*Alligators **occasionally** eat manatee babies. But they mostly leave manatees alone.*

- **A.** all the time
- **B.** most of the time
- **C.** not very often

**6.** What does **threat** mean in this book?

*Humans are manatees' biggest **threat**. For example, people build along the coast. These buildings can destroy manatees' habitats.*

- **A.** something that swims
- **B.** something that helps
- **C.** something that causes harm

*Answers can be found on page 32.*

# GLOSSARY

**algae**
Tiny plantlike living things that are found in water.

**endangered**
In danger of dying out forever.

**flippers**
Flat body parts that animals use for swimming.

**habitats**
The places where animals normally live.

**herbivores**
Animals that feed on plants to live.

**mammals**
Animals that have hair and produce milk for their young.

**molars**
Flat teeth that help animals grind food.

**nurse**
To drink milk from one's mother.

**predators**
Animals that hunt and eat other animals.

**protect**
To watch over or keep safe.

# FOR MORE INFORMATION

## BOOKS

Murray, Julie. *Bottlenose Dolphins*. Minneapolis, MN: Abdo Publishing, 2026.

Murray, Tamika M. *Meet a Baby Manatee*. Minneapolis, MN: Lerner Publications, 2024.

## WEBSITES

**Britannica Kids: Manatee**
*kids.britannica.com/kids/article/manatee/353416*
Learn more about manatees at this site.

**National Geographic Kids: West Indian Manatee**
*kids.nationalgeographic.com/animals/mammals/facts/west-indian-manatee*
Learn more facts about West Indian manatees at this website.

**Publisher's note to educators and parents:** Our editors have carefully reviewed these websites to ensure that they are suitable for students. Many websites change frequently, however, and we cannot guarantee that a site's future contents will continue to meet our high standards of quality and educational value. Be advised that students should be closely supervised whenever they access the internet.

# INDEX



**Answer Key:**
1. Answers will vary; 2. Answers will vary; 3. A; 4. A; 5. C; 6. C